To: _____

From: _____

Date: _____

especially for you because...

Bible Verse ABC's

with the CobbleKids™

Illustrated by Deborah B. Cobb

Lollipop
PUBLISHING

St. Louis, MO
www.lollipoppublishing.com

For information, write Lollipop Publishing, LLC,
P.O. Box 6354, Chesterfield, Missouri 63006-6354.
www.lollipoppublishing.com

CobbleKids™ is a registered trademark of Lollipop Publishing, LLC.

Scripture taken from the *NEW AMERICAN STANDARD BIBLE*®
© Copyright The Lockman Foundation 1960, 1962, 1963, 1968,
1971, 1972, 1973, 1975, 1977.
Used by permission. (www.lockman.org)

ISBN: 0-9709793-0-4

Library of Congress Catalog Card Number: 2001089719

Cover Design and Illustrations by Deborah B. Cobb
Graphic Design by Tim Lewis

Lollipop Publishing is dedicated to bringing Christian based,
inspirational messages to children through the publication of books
and ancillary products, serving as a means to enrich the minds and
spirits of our most precious resource: our children.

First Edition
Printed in Spain
D.L.: TO-781-2001

DEDICATION...

Accept one another... — *Romans 15:7*

In the **b**eginning God created the heavens and the earth. — *Genesis 1:1*

A joyful heart makes a **C**heerful face...
— *Proverbs 15:13*

Do what is good... — *Romans 13:3*

Encourage one another... — *Hebrews 3:13*

Consider it all joy...knowing that the testing of your **f**aith produces endurance.
— *James 1:2&3*

Blessed are the gentle, for they shall inherit the earth. — *Matthew 5:5*

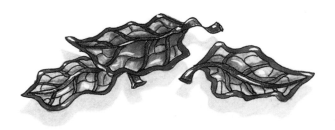

Love the Lord your God
with all your **h**eart... — *Mark 12:30*

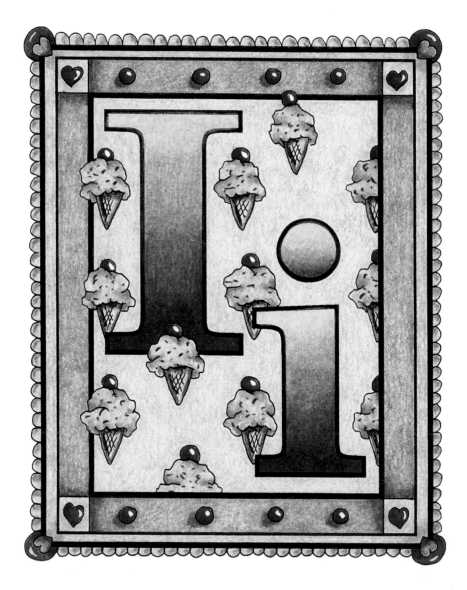

I will **i**nstruct you and teach you...
— *Psalm 32:8*

But the fruit of the Spirit is love, joy, peace, patience... — *Galatians 5:22*

...**k**indness, goodness, faithfulness, gentleness, self control; against such things there is no law. — *Galatians 5:22&23*

Love one another... — 1 John 4:7

...singing and making **m**elody with your heart to the Lord... — *Ephesians 5:19*

Draw near to God and He will draw near to you... — *James 4:8*

Children, **O**bey your parents in the Lord, for this is right.
— *Ephesians 6:1*

Love is **patient**, love is kind...
— *1 Corinthians 13:4*

Be beautiful inside, in your hearts, with the lasting charm of a gentle and quiet spirit which is so precious to God. — *1 Peter 3:4*

"Bird Seed"

Rejoice always. — *1 Thessalonians 5:16*

And do not forget to do good and to Share... — *Hebrews 13:16*

It is good to give **t**hanks to the Lord...

— *Psalm 92:1*

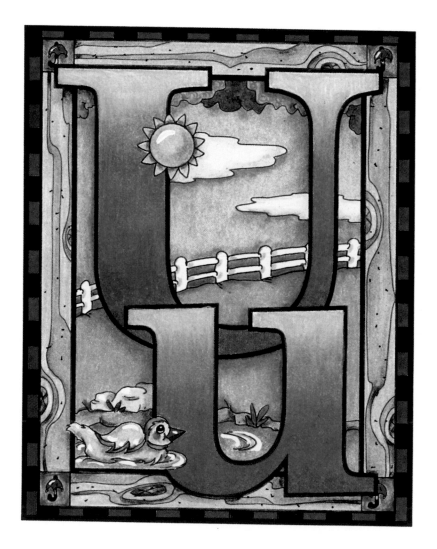

...for the Lord will give you **U**nderstanding in everything. — *2 Timothy 2:7*

Indeed the **V**ery hairs of your head are all numbered... — *Luke 12:7*

...for we **W**alk by faith, not by sight... — *2 Corinthians 5:7*

Don't let anyone look down on you because you are young, but set an eXample...in speech, in life, in love, in faith and in purity. — *1 Timothy 4:12*

For I know the plans I have for You, says the Lord. They are plans for good and not for evil, to give You a future and a hope. — *Jeremiah 29:11*

"Come with me and see my **Z**eal for the Lord."... — *2 Kings 10:16*

To Ed,

for your never-ending encouragement, love and prayers...
for letting me dream ALL my dreams! I love you BIG!

To Mom and Dad,

for your undying support of my dreams...
for your love and your prayers all my life! All my love!
(A heart full of gratitude to my "entire" loving family
and to my friends for the "years" of encouragement and support!)

To Jon and Susan,

for believing BEYOND words in CobbleKids...
for your endless energy and on-going prayers! I love you guys!

To Tim,

for your gentle spirit, talent and dedication to excellence...
I am deeply grateful!

Jeremiah 29:11

Thank you, Lord, for being Lord of my life...
for my hope is truly in you! I love you with all my heart!

is the charitable foundation
of Lollipop Pulbishing, LLC
and is the recipient of a portion of book
sales revenue, with proceeds benefiting
literacy programs and campaigns
throughout the nation.

Visit www.starforkids.org
for more information.

CobbleKids™ created by Deborah B. Cobb

www.cobblekids.com